Jelly and Bean are on the path.

They are going to the pond.

They see a red spotty cloth on the path. The cloth moves.

Jelly and Bean jump up.

Jelly thinks a big rat is under the red spotty cloth.

Bean thinks a kitten is under the red spotty cloth.

Bean pulls the cloth.

It is stuck.

He pulls the cloth again.

It is still stuck.

Then Jelly pulls the cloth with Bean. Pull … pull … pull.

The cloth comes off.

It is a hedgehog.

"Thank you for helping me," said the hedgehog. "I have been under the cloth all day."

Jelly puts the red spotty cloth on Bean. They all go to the pond.